WELCOME TO HEBREW

with SESAME STREET

J. P. PRESS

Lerner Publications ◆ Minneapolis

Dear Parents and Educators,

From its very beginning, *Sesame Street* has promoted mutual respect and cultural understanding by featuring a cast of diverse and lovable characters. *Welcome to Hebrew* introduces children to the wonderful, wide world we live in. In this book *Sesame Street* friends present handy and fun vocabulary in a language kids may not know. These words can help young readers welcome new friends. Have fun as you explore!

Sincerely,

The Editors at Sesame Workshop

Table of Contents

WELCOME!

בְּרוּךְ הַבָּא!
(Say ba-RUKH
ha-BA)

4

How to Speak Hebrew

Did you know that the Hebrew alphabet uses different letters? You read it from right to left. Practice speaking Hebrew! Each word is broken up into separate sounds called syllables. Do you see the syllable in CAPITAL LETTERS? That's the sound that you emphasize the most!

Hello.

שָׁלוֹם.

sha-LOM

This is Avigail.
She lives in Israel.

What is your name?

אֵיךְ קוֹרְאִים לָךְ?

EYKH kor-IM lach?

My name is . . .

קוֹרְאִים לִי . . .

kor-IM LI . . .

7

friendship
חֲבֵרוּת
kha-ve-RUT

best friends
חֲבֵרִים הֲכִי טוֹבִים
kha-ve-REEM
ha-KHI to-VEEM

Will you be my friend?

רוֹצֶה לִהְיוֹת חָבֵר שֶׁלִּי?

ro-TZE li-HYOT
kha-VER she-LI

dad
אַבָּא
A-ba

mom
אִמָּא
EE-ma

brother
אָח
AKH

sister
אָחוֹת
a-KHOT

grandma
סַבְתָּא
SAV-ta

grandpa
סַבָּא
SA-ba

Thank you.

תּוֹדָה.

toe-DA

Please.
בְּבַקָשָׁה.
be-va-ka-SHA

I'm sorry.
אֲנִי מִצְטַעֵר.
a-NI mitz-ta-ER

breakfast
אֲרוּחַת בּוֹקֶר
a-ru-KHAT
BO-ker

lunch
אֲרוּחַת צָהֳרַיִם
a-ru-KHAT
tzo-ha-RA-im

dinner
אֲרוּחַת עֶרֶב
a-ru-KHAT
eh-rev

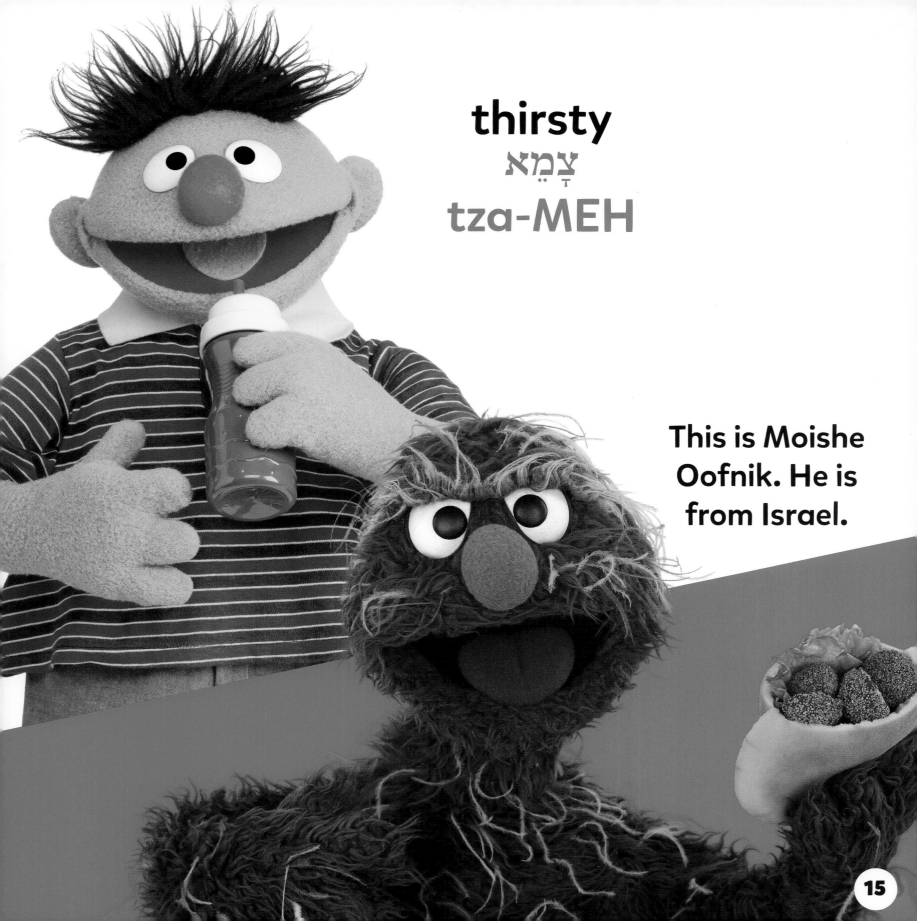

thirsty
צָמֵא
tza-MEH

This is Moishe Oofnik. He is from Israel.

How are you?
מָה שְׁלוֹמְךָ?
MA shlom-KHA

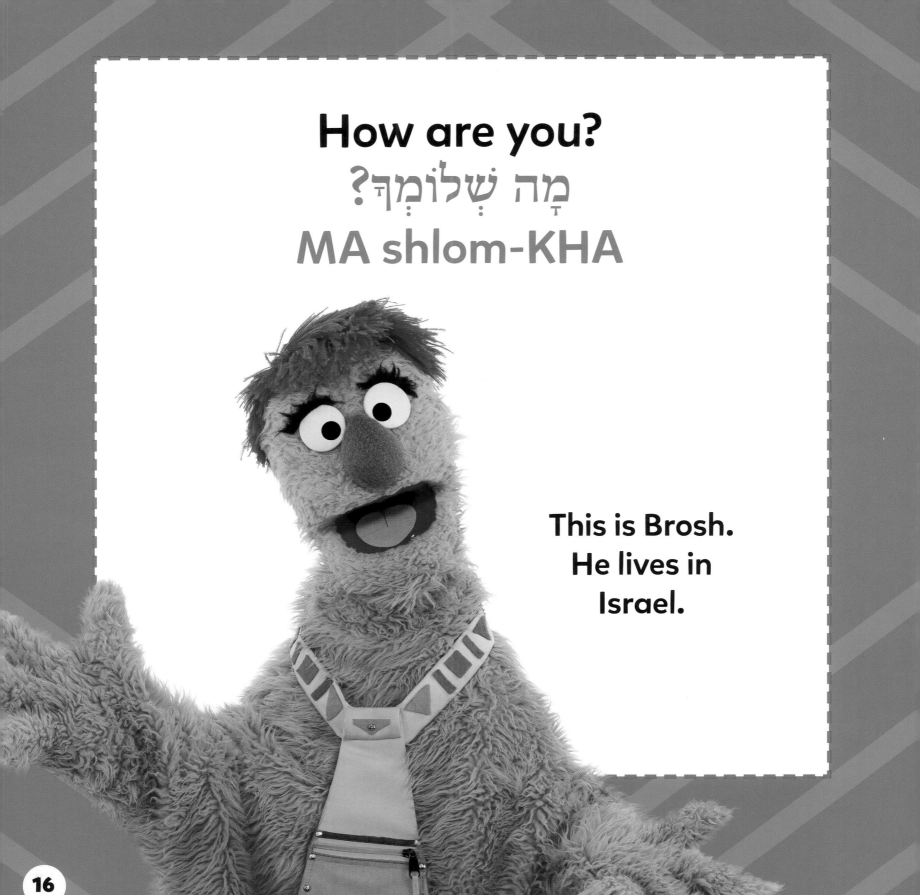

This is Brosh.
He lives in
Israel.

I'm fine, thank you.

אֲנִי בְּסֵדֶר תּוֹדָה.

a-NI be-SE-der to-DA

I like you.

אֲנִי מְחַבֵּב אוֹתְךָ.

a-NI me-kha-BEV
ot-KHA

17

happy
שָׂמֵחַ
sa-MEH-akh

I feel grumpy.
אֲנִי מַרְגִּישׁ עַצְבָּנִי.

proud

גֵּאֶה

geh-EH

excited

נִרְגָּשׁ

nir-GASH

19

dog
כֶּלֶב
KEH-lev

animals
חַיּוֹת
kha-YOT

fish
דָג
DAG

bird
צִיפּוֹר
tzi-POR

cat
חָתוּל
kha-TUL

Let's look at colors!
בּוֹא נִסְתַּכֵּל עַל צְבָעִים!

My favorite color is . . .
הַצֶּבַע הָאָהוּב עָלַי הוּא . . .
ha-TZE-va ha-a-HUV
a-LAI HU . . .

red
אָדוֹם
a-DOM

orange
כָּתוֹם
ka-TOM

yellow
צָהוֹב
tza-HOV

green
יָרוֹק
ya-ROK

blue
כָּחוֹל
ka-KHOL

purple
סָגוֹל
sa-GOL

What do you like to do?

מָה אַתָּה אוֹהֵב לַעֲשׂוֹת?

MA a-TA o-HEV
la-a-SOT

toys

צַעֲצוּעִים

tza-a-tzu-IM

jump
לִקְפּוֹץ
lik-POTZ

Let's play!
בּוֹא נְשַׂחֵק!

**Meet Sivan.
She lives in Israel.**

Goodbye.
לְהִתְרָאוֹת.
le-hit-ra-OT

See you soon!
נִתְרָאֶה בְּקָרוֹב!
nit-ra-EH be-ka-ROV

Count It!

1 **one**
אַחַת
a-KHAT

2 **two**
שְׁתַּיִם
SHTA-im

3 **three**
שָׁלוֹשׁ
sha-LOSH

4 four
אַרְבַּע
AR-ba

5 five
חָמֵשׁ
kha-MESH

6 six
שֵׁשׁ
SHESH

7 seven
שֶׁבַע
SHEH-va

8 eight
שְׁמוֹנֶה
SHMO-ne

9 nine
תֵּשַׁע
TE-sha

10 ten
עֶשֶׂר
EH-ser

Cookie Monster's Favorite Words

Are you
hungry?
אַתָּה רָעֵב?

Yummy!
טָעִים!
ta-IM

snack
חֲטִיף
kha-TIF

cookies
עוּגִיּוֹת
u-gi-YOT

30

Further Information

Admont, Shelley. *I Love to Keep my Room Clean: English Hebrew Bilingual Edition.* Kid Kiddos, 2018.

Free Hebrew Games
http://freehebrewgames.com/

Hello-World: Hebrew
http://www.hello-world.com/languages.php/?language=Hebrew

Kafka, Rebecca. *Alef is for Abba.* Minneapolis: Kar-Ben, 2014.

My First Words at Home (Hebrew/English). Cambridge, MA: Star Bright Books, 2015.

Sesame Street
http://www.sesamestreet.org

Lerner Publications Company
An imprint of Lerner Publishing Group, Inc.
241 First Avenue North
Minneapolis, MN 55401 USA

For reading levels and more information, look up this title at www.lernerbooks.com.

Main body text set in Mikado.
Typeface provided by HVD.

Additional image credits: ESB Professional/Shutterstock.com, p. 20 (dog); clarst5/Shutterstock.com, p. 20 (bird); Eric Isselee/Shutterstock.com, p. 20 (cat); Gunnar Pippel/Shutterstock.com, p. 20 (fish); Super Prin/Shutterstock.com, p. 23 (butterfly); oksana2010/Shutterstock.com, pp. 28, 29 (flower).

Library of Congress Cataloging-in-Publication Data

Names: Press, J. P., 1993– author. | Children's Television Workshop, contributor.
Title: Welcome to Hebrew with Sesame Street / J. P. Press.
Other titles: Sesame Street (Television program)
Description: Minneapolis : Lerner Publications, 2019. | Series: Sesame Street welcoming words | Includes bibliographical references.
Identifiers: LCCN 2018059304 (print) | LCCN 2019009700 (ebook) | ISBN 9781541562509 (eb pdf) | ISBN 9781541555013 (lb : alk. paper) | ISBN 9781541574953 (pb : alk. paper)
Subjects: LCSH: Hebrew language—Conversation books and phrase books—English—Juvenile literature.
Classification: LCC PJ4573 (ebook) | LCC PJ4573 .P74 2019 (print) | DDC 492.4/83421—dc23

LC record available at https://lccn.loc.gov/2018059304

Manufactured in the United States of America
1-45826-42703-3/7/2019